To

# voices
## *of* prayer

MORNING,
EVENING,
& ALWAYS

*Let us pray for each other !*
*With thanks & love,*
*Janet*

TWENTY
THIRD 23rd
PUBLICATIONS
www.23rdpublications.com

The prayers for this book are taken from *Living Faith: Daily Catholic Devotions*, a publication of Creative Communications for the Parish.

TWENTY-THIRD PUBLICATIONS
A Division of Bayard
One Montauk Avenue, Suite 200
New London, CT 06320
(860) 437-3012 or (800) 321-0411
www.23rdpublications.com

ISBN 978-1-58595-737-8
Library of Congress Catalog Card Number: 2008944169

Printed in the U.S.A.

# CONTENTS

## Traditional Catholic Prayers

# ▰ INTRODUCTION ▰

In the classic movie *It's a Wonderful Life*, the people of the fictional town of Bedford Falls pray fervently to God to help their friend George Bailey. In this memorable scene, the prayers of the townsfolk soar to the heavens against a backdrop of a beautifully clear starlit night. It is an endearing and powerful image of ordinary people using ordinary words to speak to God.

Perhaps our notion of prayer resembles this Hollywood version, simply talking to God as we would to a dear, dear friend. That's how the great spiritual writer Henri Nouwen envisioned prayer, calling it a "conversation with God." Isn't that what we want? To be able to talk with someone who loves us completely, someone who knows us more intimately than we can ever comprehend, someone who understands our fears, our desires, our dreams. That is our hope for this book.

*Voices of Prayer* is a response to the many loyal readers who have requested copies of our prayers, which appear in back of each edition of *Living Faith*. From a trove of hundreds that have been published over the years, we endeavored to choose the best of the best. We have arranged the prayers loosely around the Church's liturgical year, with several pages of morning and evening prayers and prayers for special intentions. In the back of the book are traditional Catholic prayers. We hope you enjoy this volume and that it becomes not only a companion but a "conversation" starter with God.

*Paul P. Pennick*
Editor

# ADVENT

❧ Lord Jesus, you came to bring us the fullness of joy and to free us from all the pale imitations of happiness. This Advent, remove any barriers we have put up to keep you out of our lives. Teach us to welcome your presence wherever we find it, even in the difficulties and challenges of daily life. As we reach out in love to others, especially the poor and needy, may we come to know in our hearts that we are welcoming you, our Lord and Savior. *Amen.*

❧ Light of the World, enter the darkness of our hearts and renew us in faith, hope, and love. As we prepare to celebrate the great mystery of the Incarnation, help us to see your presence in our world, especially in the needs of the poor. Strengthen us to become true peacemakers able to love our enemies and forgive those who have offended us. Lead us to acknowledge our own sinfulness, accept your mercy, and extend your healing love to those around us. *Amen.*

# Morning

🔷 Lord, I start a bit slower on these cold winter mornings. But as the sun peeks through the clouds, it reminds me of the warmth of your embrace. With your help, dear Lord, may I spend this day in praise of your creation, in praise of your goodness, in praise of your mercy and forgiveness. *Amen.*

🔷 Dear Lord, you give me another day of life, a treasure that I too often ignore. Give me the strength to acknowledge your infinite generosity and goodness. Show me the way this day to express my gratitude for all you have given me. Help me share this bounty with those in need. *Amen.*

🔷 I arise, Almighty, and search for your light. Raise my eyes to the heavens, and lift my spirit to praise you. Carry me in the palm of your hand, and hold me close, for you are the Most High. *Amen.*

# Evening

My day has ended, dear Lord. As sleep approaches, I thank you for keeping my loved ones in your care this day. I pray for a peaceful night's rest and a peaceful world this night. Please forgive my sins and help me to begin my day tomorrow with a heart filled with love to do your will. *Amen.*

Dear Lord, with another day about to end, make me be attentive to your voice. Calm my restless spirit; bring peace to my heart. Help me realize that whatever I accomplish it could not be done without your unending gifts of grace. *Amen.*

Jesus, quiet my heart as another day draws to a close. Where I have been able to serve you well, I give thanks for the presence of your Spirit in my heart. Where I have failed to respond to the promptings of that same Spirit, I ask your pardon. Help me to let go of the day's concerns and place my trust fully in you throughout the night. Whether wakeful or asleep, may I never lack for confidence in your mercy and love. *Amen.*

# *Christmas prayer*

Mighty and Eternal God, Power of the Universe, you came among us as an infant to set us free from fear. Sharing our life, you shared also our destiny, accepting death on our behalf. As we celebrate the wonderful mystery of God-With-Us, help us to see the value of our lives from your point of view. May we cherish all human life and support one another as we journey together toward our final destiny in you. Grant us a share of your love that we might more fully love one another. *Amen.*

# New Year

Lord, thank you for bringing me to a new year. During the days ahead, help me to know your presence, see your love at work, and live always in the light of the event that has changed forever all space and time—the coming of your Son, Jesus. May I remain aware each day of this new year that I am your beloved child. *Amen.*

# A winter prayer

Lord, you bring the cold winds with the gentle rains. Before the earth springs into new life, you give it a season of stillness and death. Silence the voices of busyness in our hearts, and open our ears to hear your voice. In Christ's name, *Amen.*

# Morning

❃ As the rising sun makes its presence known, Lord, show me your face as well. Fill me with your peace and love, so that I can shine with your light wherever I go. Help me to always remain open to the wisdom of your Holy Spirit, and guide my hands and feet so that they might lead others to you. *Amen.*

❃ Lord, your sacred powers never cease to amaze me. May I always remember that you have given me the ability to serve you each day. When I fail to see where my talents are needed, give me the dawn of another opportunity. When I am too weak to follow through, give me the strength to go on faithfully tomorrow. When I refuse you, give me mercy and melt my heart of stone. I pray this in the name of Jesus. *Amen.*

❃ Lord, make me ready to do your will. Give me strength and courage, love and patience to accept the day's trials as well as its blessings. May I never dismiss the gentle promptings of your Spirit. If I do, call me by name until my heart returns to you. I pray for those who need you most, especially those I encounter today. *Amen.*

# Evening

⚫ Gentle Jesus, come to me in my time of rest. Fill my heart with peace, and save me from the threat of death, from the empty promises of the devil who waits to tempt me. Remain with those who are in my heart, and teach me to speak to them in only your love. *Amen.*

⚫ Jesus, help me tonight to be still and silent in mind, body, and spirit, so that I might hear and take to heart the words faith tells me the heavenly Father whispers to me constantly: "You are my beloved." *Amen.*

⚫ Light of the World, Star Ever-Shining, at the end of the day you say to me, "Do not be afraid." But the powerful are threatening, and the poor are in tears. Rescue us, Savior, for we rest only in you. Do not leave us in our own weak hands, but comfort us and hide us in the shadow of your wings. Repair any damage we caused today in action or in idleness, and grant us the peace and joy that comes with the dawn of hope. *Amen.*

❧ Lord, you endured forty days of temptation and suffering. Lead me into the desert as you did the children of Israel. Change my contrite heart, and help me grow in holiness. Guide my steps of sacrifice to Calvary and beyond the empty tomb. May I rise with you on Easter to a new life of grace. I ask this in your name. *Amen.*

❧ Lord Jesus, you were put to death by my offenses, raised on the cross for my guilt! You were slapped that I might be touched by your healing hand! You were tormented that I might be comforted, harassed that I might hope, crowned with thorns that I might be crowned with glory. Jesus, may I be grateful for your love that is beyond understanding. *Amen.*

# For Holy Week

🔹 Holy Spirit, help us this week to dwell
reverently and gratefully on the mystery of the
redemptive cross of Christ. We are tempted to be
overwhelmed by the horror of the Cross. Yet how
can we not be in awe of this mysterious event, of
God's very own Son undergoing a painful and
shameful death to bring life? Open our hearts to
this mystery of divine love and mercy, and give
us renewed appreciation of it. *Amen.*

🔹 O God, I do not understand why any suffering
is necessary, much less the suffering of one
innocent like Jesus. Give me the consolation
inspired by faith and bolstered by prayer to
understand that had your Kingdom of Love been
able to grow without suffering, you would have
chosen that way. *Amen.*

🔹 O God, may our prayer and meditation on Jesus'
suffering and death be not only an exercise
in stirring up pious feelings, but also a firm
commitment on our part to live the life of true
discipleship by taking up our cross and following
him. *Amen.*

# Morning

✤ Lord, I rise in gratitude for the gift of another day. As the concerns of the day begin to flood my mind, I offer them to you, and I pray that your Spirit will lead me to serve you in all things. May I be aware of your presence today, especially in any temptations or trials I may face. For your greater glory, I pray in Jesus' name. *Amen.*

✤ Lord Jesus, fill me with a desire to remain in your presence through everything that happens today. May I find you in the people I encounter and the events that take place. When I have a quiet moment, may I turn to you in prayer. May I trust in your love and care whether I am aware of it or not. I know you hold all things in your hands, and I pray to be firm in that confidence at every moment. *Amen.*

# *Evening*

✠ Jesus, thank you for the gift of this day, even in its burdens and failures. For what I have done wrong or failed to do well, I ask your mercy. Confident that you have forgiven me, may I put aside any regrets, sadness, or shame and simply bask in the warmth of your love. Give me the wisdom to trust in your everlasting love for me and for those I love. *Amen.*

✠ Thank you, Lord, for the goodness of this day. I was not always aware of your presence. But you were there. For those times I drifted away from your Spirit within me, I am sorry. I hope tomorrow, and all my tomorrows, will be filled with a more lively sense of your will for me. Give me a good night's sleep so that I can rise in the morning refreshed and with renewed faith, hope, and love. *Amen.*

O God, show me your hidden presence in my life that I may know the glory of your resurrection and "no longer search for the living among the dead." Give me a firm confidence that you are with me and guiding me along the way to full union with you in heaven. *Amen.*

Risen Lord, we rejoice in your glorious triumph over sin and death as we celebrate this season of Easter. May the new life of forgiveness that we have received from you strengthen us to forgive others and to seek reconciliation. May new life, rooted in peace and harmony, grow in our relationships at home, at school, at work. *Amen.*

O Risen Lord, we owe you a tremendous debt of gratitude for taking the weight of sin on yourself to set us free. Your triumph over the grave has given us a new life. Help us to accept the path of discipleship and follow you daily for the sake of love. May we remember that through your sacrifice, the power of sin and death has been overcome by your transforming love. *Amen.*

❧ O Risen Lord, in this Easter season may the Holy Spirit deepen my awareness of the mystery of salvation and increase my appreciation of all God's gifts. *Amen.*

❧ Lord, I thank you for all you are and do. Your generosity has no limits. Created reality of matter and spirit is rich beyond my wildest imagination, and then beyond that lavish feast of creation comes your even more lavish feast of redemption, capped by the Resurrection and the promise of eternal happiness in heaven with you. Thank you, thank you. *Amen.*

❧ God of all life, we rejoice with you in the day of death's defeat. To the bewildered eyes of your disciples, Christ's death looked like tragic loss, but you turned it into a great gain. Give us the faith you gave them to believe that, through the creative power of your love, even the greatest tragedy can be transformed and become life-giving. May our faith grow throughout the fifty days of this Easter season as we pray to embrace your gift of new and everlasting life. *Amen.*

# Morning

❇ Lord Jesus Christ, may this day bring justice to the oppressed, health to the sick, and relief to those lands aflame with war and hatred. Help me to be an instrument of your peace. *Amen.*

❇ More certain than the sunrise is your salvation, Lord. Right now I do not see things clearly, but I pray that as your Light increases, I will detect the path you have set in front of me. Grant me the courage to walk in the darkness. With each step, may I grow closer to you. *Amen.*

❇ Lord, this day is a greater gift than I can imagine. At every turn I will encounter your blessings, and every moment will give me a chance to praise you. I know there may be times of sadness and confusion, but even these will be opportunities to trust in you. I pray for that trust. Thank you for being with me in everything I do. *Amen.*

# Evening

✺ Jesus, help me to let go of my cares and frustrations so I can surrender to your embrace in the loving arms of sleep. *Amen.*

✺ Lord, give me repose. Lead me by restful waters and verdant pastures. Fill my cup by morning's light, and let me enter into your kingdom when all my days are through, for you are my shepherd and all that I want. *Amen.*

✺ I am tired, Lord, and there is much about this day that I don't understand. I wanted to do the right thing, but it seems to have eluded me. I trust that you will show me what I need to know at the right time. I pray for wisdom that I may be alert to your presence in my life and that I may always follow your path. Give me the rest I need for the challenges of tomorrow. *Amen.*

# Pentecost

Holy Spirit, enlighten me with your truth, guide me with your understanding, strengthen me with your courage, console me with your love, and keep me secure in hope. *Amen.*

# For the Church

Guide and protect your Church, O Lord, as you have promised to do. May the Church be bold in proclaiming the Good News of Christ, and may it be firm in teaching all the sacred truths entrusted to it. Above all, may we, the Church, strive always to be humble and repentant, realizing that while on our pilgrimage here we only see "darkly as through a glass" (1 Cor 13:12) and will only know you fully in eternity when we are united in heaven as the Church triumphant. *Amen.*

## For wisdom

Lord, you have given me your Holy Spirit
to guide me toward all that is true and good
and right. Help me amid life's confusions and
contradictions to listen carefully to your voice
within me. Help me to accept the truth of
my situation, even if that sometimes means
accepting uncertainty and ambiguity. Help me to
trust that you will bring all things to completion
when the time is right. *Amen.*

## For fidelity

O God, I know how to make excuses for myself
and to pardon my behavior when I am clearly
in the wrong. But I also know very well that
happiness cannot be based on lies. Send me your
grace that I might be faithful to the gospel and
to the commitments I have made as a Catholic. I
know you will lead me to joy, not sorrow, and so
I place my trust in you. *Amen.*

# *Morning*

❧ Lord, every day you give me is a good day, but sometimes I forget that and start the day with a grumble instead of gratitude. Today I want to praise you for all the goodness of your creation. May I treasure these moments today, never taking them for granted. May I serve you and my neighbor with energy and good cheer. *Amen.*

❧ Lord, as this day begins afresh with new light, you have given me rest and renewed me with a night of sleep. In gratitude I begin this new day with hope. May I take a path that is worthy of your gift of new life. I know I have choices to make, Lord, and I pray that you will help me always choose out of love. And when I fail, may I give you thanks when you bring it to my attention. *Amen.*

❧ Lord, one thing I need from you today is strength. With so much to do, I need to be at my best. You have given me the desire to face this day with courage, and I know you will always be with me. May I have faith to know you are near. Please give me a sense that you are at my side— and on my side—in all that I do this day. *Amen.*

# *Evening*

🌸 Almighty God, I now let go of all that has happened today. Where I have failed you, I ask your pardon. Where you have given me success or blessing, I thank you. Most of all I am grateful for the gift of life and now for the chance to rest. I place my trust in you tonight and ask for one more gift: a good night's sleep. *Amen.*

🌸 Lord Jesus, be with me now as I prepare for sleep. Grant me peace of mind and an open heart to receive the rest that I need. Bless my loved ones as I entrust them to your care. May they know they are loved by me, and even more by you. May they be free of all worry this night. May they thank you in good times and call upon you in their trials. *Amen.*

🌸 Lord God, now that the day is finished, I thank you once more for the gift of life. May I surrender to sleep in the full confidence of your abiding love for me. *Amen.*

## For a sense of humor

Help me to laugh at myself, Lord, especially in my frustration and impatience. Allow me to find the simple joy of a good laugh, even in the midst of hard work and serious concerns. Cleanse my joking of any sarcasm or bitterness. Remind me today and every day that you have made us for joy. *Amen.*

## For compassion

Lord, when my heart is hardened, help me to remember how many people have cared for me over the years. When I am judgmental, remind me of all the mercy I have enjoyed. When I just don't care what others are suffering because they're different, far away, or unworthy, touch my heart and soul with the compassion that brought Jesus all the way to the cross for me. *Amen.*

## For a forgiving heart

Lord, anger and hurt have turned my heart to stone. Help me to remember how often you have forgiven me. Give me the desire to forgive and the hope of true healing. *Amen.*

## For humility

O God, you have made us out of earth, so let me be content with being human. Your breath has given us life, so let me gratefully receive the divine spark within my soul. Help me to accept the truth of who I really am, loved into being and sent to serve humbly in your name. *Amen.*

# *Morning*

✦ Lord Jesus, I thank you for the night's rest. As I organize the day's schedule, open my ears to your voice, and help me to hear what you are calling me to do today. *Amen.*

✦ Holy Spirit, I thank you for another opportunity to share the gifts you have given me. As I begin this day, open my eyes to your presence here on earth and help me to take the time to help others along the way. *Amen.*

✦ Good morning, God! Please give me the strength to do the tasks that you set before me today. Whenever I find myself with a bit of extra time, prompt my heart to pray for those who are working without the luxury of a spare moment. In the midst of personal challenges, I often become self-absorbed and forget your many blessings. Guide me toward a sincere appreciation of the trust you have in my abilities, and move me to use them for the benefit of my neighbors. *Amen.*

# Evening

✣ Heavenly Father, I thank you for another day. As the world interrupts my dreams, open my heart to your love, and help me to spend this day in joyful praise of your creation. *Amen.*

✣ Lord, forgive me for failing today to make the most of the opportunities you gave me to grow in love and holiness. Some of those opportunities I didn't even recognize until it was too late, while others I rejected out of hand because of my hardness of heart. Open my heart and mind that I may respond more faithfully tomorrow to my high calling to know, love, and serve you, and to love others as I love myself. *Amen.*

✣ Jesus, you spent the night in prayer so that I might spend the night at rest. Grant me that rest tonight, but if I am wakeful, remind me that you also asked your disciples to watch and pray with you. Then help me to join with you in a vigil of prayer for the needs of the world, and especially my loved ones. *Amen.*

# A prayer for peace

Almighty God, you alone are the source of true peace in the world and in the human heart. Free us from the grip of violence, war, and hatred. Show us a better way of solving our problems and of living together as one people. Heal us all of the damage caused by the bombs and bullets—and the willingness to use them against the innocent. *Amen.*

# For the country

Almighty God, thank you for this country. I often fail to see how blessed we are. Thank you for the opportunities that have allowed us to achieve so much for so many. Thank you for the yet-untapped material and spiritual resources that hold the rich potential for even greater achievements. May we accept these gifts in deep gratitude and use them for good. *Amen.*

# *For peace and those who protect us*

O God, giver of life, watch over and protect the fathers and mothers, wives and husbands, who are members of our Armed Forces. Be with them when they wake in the morning, and let them sleep peacefully at the end of each day. Guide them as they travel over land, sea, and in the air. Keep them and their families safe, and hasten their return to us.

We also ask you to protect the innocent, especially children and the elderly, in places torn apart by war, hatred, and violence. Send your Spirit of Peace into the hearts of us all, so that the day may come soon when we can live together side by side, creating ways to help one another rather than looking for ways to hurt each other. *Amen.*

# Morning

✤ Lord, you will be present to me with all your healing and redemptive power at every moment of this day. Help me to know your healing presence, to appreciate it, and to live in it joyfully and prayerfully today and every day of my life. *Amen.*

✤ Lord, may I begin this new day in heartfelt gratitude for your gift of life and for your gift of faith, hope, and love that is the only true and trustworthy source of my happiness and peace. May my gratitude for your gifts not just flame up quickly within me and fade, but rather spur me throughout this day to share joyfully with others your many gifts. *Amen.*

✤ Lord, already at the start of this new day my heart has been burdened with worries and anxieties about a host of things. Help me to back up and start over, this time with a profoundly peaceful awareness of your divine love that will banish all my worries and anxieties. May I start—and end—this day resting in your peace. *Amen.*

# Evening

❁ Lord, I regret the times today that I sought you in the wrong places and for the wrong reasons. Help me tomorrow to pursue you and the things that come from you, because that pursuit is the only worthwhile pursuit. Help me make the right choices so that I learn to value the things that will draw me into loving accord with your will, for it is in union with you through the pursuit of your will that I will find my true happiness. *Amen.*

❁ Lord, you have extended to me the gift of your friendship, the most priceless treasure imaginable. Help me understand and appreciate more fully the nature of this gift—and what it demands of me. May I rest tonight in the peace and security of your friendship and, when tomorrow comes, may I begin anew to grow in my friendship with you. *Amen.*

# A prayer for life

God of all creation, all life and all meaning come from you. Keep us mindful of your many gifts of food and friends, of freedom and health. These are luxuries in many places. With your Holy Spirit, make me an agent of life and peace in the world. Give me the courage to live according to your truth as an example for others to follow. *Amen.*

# For gracious words

O Lord, forgive me for my often loose and undisciplined tongue. Help me to grow in graciousness of speech. Save me from words that needlessly hurt others, especially from words of gossip, slander, and lies. May I speak only the truth and whatever encourages and helps others to know me and to know themselves better. *Amen.*

# *For growth in holiness*

✤ O God, you have revealed in your Son Jesus that your will for us is to be saved and to come to the full joy of union with you. Help us to root out whatever keeps us from growing in holiness and truth. Help us to see and cherish with all our hearts what will bring us closer to you each day. *Amen.*

✤ Lord, may your Church become ever more truly what it is called to be, a band of chosen servants united above all else in seeking you with their whole heart, in serving you and the gospel with all their energy and zeal, and in living lives of prayer and gratitude for all your many gifts and blessings. *Amen.*

✤ Lord, grant us, your Church, the wisdom and creativity to be good stewards of the spiritual and material wealth you have entrusted to our care. Help us to depend on your divine strength in all we do, and to acknowledge that we, like all who struggle in this tragically flawed world, must lean on your divine mercy rather than our own powers. *Amen.*

# Morning

✦ O my God, only you are God. Only you, only your holy and healing presence, provide all I need to be happy and free. Help me to begin this day in silent adoration. Help me to know what I truly treasure and desire—and if it is not you, may I begin today to make you my heart's desire. Help me to see and to judge everything by your divine light and love. *Amen.*

✦ Lord God, thank you for the gift of life. Help me to know and love you, the giver of all life. *Amen.*

✦ God of infinite love, may I be awake and attentive to your call throughout this day. Give me the desire and the discipline to respond to your call to grow in my relationship with you in all the ordinary events of this day. May I draw ever closer to you, the source of all that is good and true and holy. *Amen.*

# Evening

◆ Lord, if I dwell excessively on my sins and
failings of this day, I easily become discouraged
by my weaknesses and selfishness. Instead,
I resolve to end this day remembering the
awesome goodness, truth, and beauty revealed
in your love and mercy for us. Forgive me for
the time I spent foolishly today on trivia and
distractions. Help me to do better tomorrow.
*Amen.*

◆ Lord, I failed today to ask for and to seek the
beautiful gifts of the Holy Spirit that I need to
grow in holiness and to draw nearer to you.
Ignite the fire of the Holy Spirit within me now
so that I begin to pray for and to seek what I
truly need. *Amen.*

◆ My day has ended, dear Lord. As sleep
approaches, I thank you for keeping my loved
ones in your care this day. I pray for a peaceful
night's rest and a peaceful world. Please forgive my
sins and help me to begin my day tomorrow with
a heart filled with love to do your will. *Amen.*

# A prayer for the sick

Gracious God, your Son healed the sick and visited the lonely. Come to me now, and take away my fears and pain. Give me the strength and rest I need to recover and return to health. Help me to pray sincerely as Jesus did, "Let this cup pass from me, but not as I will, but your will be done." Amen.

# For recovery from illness

O God, thank you for bringing me through my long illness and restoring my health. Help me to show my gratitude by serving you more faithfully in my daily life, by more fervent prayer and devotion, and by sharing my time and resources more generously with others, especially those in need. Amen.

# For shut-ins

Dear Lord, we pray for all those persons who are confined to nursing homes or hospitals, unable to move freely among us. Please watch over them and protect them. If it is your will, bring them back to health, to their homes, to their families, so that they may enjoy the wonders of your creation. We ask this in your name, Christ our Savior. *Amen.*

# For those in nursing homes

Lord Jesus Christ, hope of the frail and infirm, come today to comfort and redeem all those in nursing homes, especially [name]. Help all those who devote nights and days to serving them. Give us all the grace to see your face in one another no matter where we live. *Amen.*

# Morning

🔹 Lord, may I remember today the heartfelt lament of Saint Augustine who recalled regretfully that he had sought you far and wide, but you were within him all along. Give me the grace to know you, the true God, and thereby to know myself, my true self, in you. *Amen.*

🔹 God, may I learn the humility I need to respect the profound difference between your ways and my ways, the gaps between us that my limited knowledge can never close. Help me today to adore you and to love you precisely in the dark mystery of your divine reality. *Amen.*

🔹 Lord, you provide every good gift and bless us with the overflowing abundance of the earth. You invite us to enjoy those gifts, but also to be good stewards of them. Help us today to be generous and compassionate to all who need help. May we never use our giving or service to others to pretend that we are superior to them, but rather remain humbly aware that we are no less needy in our own ways. *Amen.*

# *Evening*

✣ O God, I ask your blessing on my rest from the work and the anxieties of this day. Let me sleep in peace knowing that my loved ones are safe in your care. For what I have done wrong today, forgive me—and give me peace that comes from knowing your forgiveness. Let me awake refreshed for the tasks of tomorrow. I ask this in Jesus' name. *Amen.*

✣ Loving God, you are the giver of life and the source of all strength. Help me tonight to forgive everyone and everything that I feel have hurt me so that I begin now to live fully as your joyful child. *Amen.*

✣ Lord, as I look back upon the day, show me your hand in the blessings I enjoyed. Reveal yourself in the simple joys of a cool drink or a gentle breeze. Remind me that you were present even in moments of distress when I felt uncomfortable, frightened, or angry. Teach me how I might have acted better so that when the opportunity comes again, I might love others more as you do. I give you thanks for every good thing and ask your blessing on my rest tonight. *Amen.*

# For thanksgiving

✥ O God, thank you for the many material and spiritual blessings you have lavished on us. May we learn to enjoy them, to delight in them, and to appreciate them fully without being possessed by them. May the gifts we've been given lead us ever closer to you, our hope and our true happiness. *Amen.*

✥ Giver of all good gifts, you are the source of all that we have, beginning with the gift of life itself. As we pause from our labors, we remember in gratitude that everything we enjoy can be traced back to your hand. May we never take for granted the gifts of health, family, talent, and opportunity, and may we use them for the good of all people. May we also open our hearts to find you in the gift of suffering that draws us closer to Jesus, the One who gave his life to us that we might have a share in his divine life. *Amen.*

# For healing

Gracious Lord, remember in your mercy those who suffer today. Give strength and encouragement to those who minister to their needs.

Remember your promise not to let them be tested beyond what they are able to bear. Above all, give them the reassurance that you are with them as they walk through this valley of the shadows of death. And in your good time send healing of body and spirit. (Name those who need healing or help in their suffering.) In Jesus' name. *Amen.*

# Morning

❧ Lord, many hundreds of things from the urgent to the trivial will come and go in my life today, making it easy for me to forget the really important truths of my faith and, perhaps, even to neglect what I should do to stay close to you and live in your presence. May my prayerful awareness and reflection during this day help me to keep you first in my mind and heart. *Amen.*

❧ Lord, all of Scripture gives profound witness to the one great truth that each of us, indeed the whole universe, was created out of your overflowing love. May we open our hearts to your divine love today—and so come to know you and ourselves a little more fully than we did yesterday. *Amen.*

❧ God, you are our hope in this life and the next. Out of infinite love you created, redeemed, and called us to holiness. May we live today—and each day—in grateful appreciation of your love. May all we do and say work not only for our own sanctification and happiness, but also for the health, holiness, and happiness of others who will be with us today. *Amen.*

# *Evening*

✦ Lord, my heart is heavy tonight when I think of all the opportunities I missed today to draw near to you. But I will not focus on me, but rather on you. For in you is the hope that banishes despair, the strength that overcomes weakness, and the joy that tempers sadness. Renew my resolve to live a life faithful to your grace. *Amen.*

✦ Lord, give me the Spirit of wisdom and understanding, the Spirit of counsel and strength, the Spirit of knowledge and holy fear and profound respect for you. May I ever seek your face with all my heart, with all my soul, and with all my mind. Give me a contrite and humble spirit. May I cherish your love. *Amen.*

✦ Dear Lord, with another day about to end, make me be attentive to your voice. Calm my restless spirit; bring peace to my heart. Help me realize that whatever I accomplish it could not be done without your unending gifts of grace. *Amen.*

# For teenagers

O Lord, bless all the young who are growing up in this world. They are the promise of the future family, the future Church, the future world. Guide their idealism and energy, their need to take their lives into their own hands as adults, their openness to the rich variety of your creation. Give them confidence, hope, and gentle hearts. Protect them from discouragement and cynicism, and from counterfeit values. Give them, above all, the courage to take up their responsibilities, the wisdom to absorb the best of the past, and the happiness that comes from faith in you. *Amen.*

# For loved ones away from home

O God, enfold in your loving care all our dear ones who are away from us and all who are traveling by land, sea, or air. May your fatherly arms surround them and keep them safe. Give them the daily strength they need. Guide them into a greater faith, hope, and love for you. *Amen.*

# Upon retirement

Ever-living God, you have called us all to a
life of faithfulness. Thank you for the talents,
opportunities, and strength you bestowed on me.
Grant me the wisdom and courage to serve you
in new ways, in new places, and in the peace that
comes from you. May I always trust that you will
continue to give me all that I need. *Amen.*

# For a happy death

O God of the living and the dead, we are to
appear before you after this short life to render
an account of how well we used the many gifts
you gave us. Help us now to prepare for our
last hour, and protect us against a sudden and
unprovided death. Help us to always live in
the ways of your commandments. Teach us to
"watch and pray," so that when your summons
comes for our departure from this world, we may
go forth to meet you and experience a merciful
judgment. We ask this through Christ our Lord.
*Amen.*

# Morning

✠ Loving God, make us aware today of the many fears that may be preventing us from seeking to know, love, and serve you more faithfully. Instill in us a liberating love that casts out our fears and dreads, and opens our minds and hearts to you and to all our sisters and brothers in Christ. *Amen.*

✠ Jesus, renew in me the spirit of prayer, contemplation, and solitude that serves to draw me ever nearer to you and helps me to rest quietly, calmly, and confidently in your presence. Increase my longing for you, and help me to cherish and make the most of those precious moments of silent prayer and praise that will come my way today. *Amen.*

✠ Lord, thank you for the gift of this day, unique in its opportunities and challenges, yet filled with your everlasting love. May I accept with open hands all that you wish to give me today. May I do all things for your greater glory. *Amen.*

# *Evening*

✣ Lord, help me tonight to be still and silent in mind, body, and spirit, so that I might take to heart the words you have spoken to us through the prophet Jeremiah: "I have loved you with an everlasting love." *Amen.*

✣ Lord, into your hands I commend myself. You have been my strength and my help throughout the day. Stay with me also through this night. May a renewed awareness of your loving presence, and of your forgiveness and mercy free my heart from all the troubling worries and cares of this day. *Amen.*

✣ Lord, you search my heart and so you know my worries and fears as well as my joys and delights. I place all these things in your hands: the good and the bad alike. Give me the trust I need to let go of the past and to hope in the future, whether I can control that or not. May this night bring me a renewal in body, mind, and spirit so that I can rise refreshed tomorrow to do your will. *Amen.*

# TRADITIONAL
# CATHOLIC
# PRAYERS

# Sign of the Cross

In the Name of the Father, and of the Son, and of the Holy Spirit, *Amen.*

# Our Father

Our Father, Who art in Heaven, hallowed be Thy Name. Thy Kingdom come. Thy Will be done, on earth, as it is in Heaven. Give us this day our daily bread and forgive us our trespasses as we forgive those who trespass against us; and lead us not into temptation, but deliver us from evil. *Amen.*

# Hail Mary

Hail Mary, full of grace, the Lord is with thee.
Blessed art thou among women, and blessed is
the fruit of thy womb, Jesus.
Holy Mary, Mother of God, pray for us sinners,
now, and at the hour of our death. *Amen.*

# Glory Be

Glory be to the Father, and to the Son, and to the
Holy Spirit, as it was in the beginning, is now,
and ever shall be, world without end. *Amen.*

# Apostles' Creed

I believe in God the Father Almighty, Creator of Heaven and earth, and in Jesus Christ, His only Son, our Lord, Who was conceived by the Holy Spirit, born of the Virgin Mary, suffered under Pontius Pilate, was crucified, died, and was buried. He descended into Hell; the third day He arose again from the dead; He ascended into Heaven and is seated at the right hand of God the Father Almighty, from thence He shall come to judge the living and the dead. I believe in the Holy Spirit, the Holy Catholic Church, the Communion of Saints, the forgiveness of sins, the resurrection of the body, and life everlasting. Amen.

# Act of Contrition

O my God, I am heartily sorry for having offended Thee, and I detest all my sins because I dread the loss of Heaven and the pains of Hell; but most of all because they offend Thee, my God, Who art all-good and deserving of all my love. I firmly resolve, with the help of Thy grace, to confess my sins, to do penance, and to amend my life. *Amen.*

# The Confiteor

I confess to Almighty God, to blessed Mary, ever Virgin, to blessed Michael the Archangel, to blessed John the Baptist, to the Holy Apostles Peter and Paul, and to all the Saints, that I have sinned exceedingly in thought, word and deed, through my fault, through my fault, through my most grievous fault. Therefore I beseech blessed Mary, ever Virgin, blessed Michael the Archangel, blessed John the Baptist, the holy Apostles Peter and Paul, and all the Saints, to pray to the Lord our God for me.

# The Divine Praises

Blessed be God.

Blessed be His holy Name.

Blessed be Jesus Christ, true God and true man.

Blessed be the Name of Jesus.

Blessed be His most Sacred Heart.

Blessed be His Precious Blood.

Blessed be Jesus in the Most Holy Sacrament of the Altar.

Blessed be the Holy Spirit, the Paraclete.

Blessed be the great Mother of God, Mary most holy.

Blessed be her holy and Immaculate Conception.

Blessed be her glorious assumption.

Blessed be the name of Mary, Virgin and Mother.

Blessed be St. Joseph, her most chaste spouse.

Blessed be God in His angels and in His saints.

May the heart of Jesus, in the Most Blessed Sacrament, be praised, adored, and loved with grateful affection, at every moment, in all the tabernacles of the world, even to the end of time. *Amen.*

# The Beatitudes

Blessed are the poor in spirit; for theirs is the kingdom of heaven.

Blessed are the meek; for they shall possess the land.

Blessed are they that mourn; for they shall be comforted.

Blessed are they that hunger and thirst after justice; for they shall be filled.

Blessed are the merciful; for they shall obtain mercy.

Blessed are the pure of heart; for they shall see God.

Blessed are the peacemakers; for they shall be called the children of God.

Blessed are they that suffer persecution for justice sake; for theirs is the kingdom of heaven.

# Anima Christi

Soul of Christ, be my sanctification;
Body of Christ, be my salvation;
Blood of Christ, fill all my veins;
Water from Christ's side, wash out my stains;
Passion of Christ, my comfort be,
O good Jesus, listen to me.
In thy wounds I fain would hide,
Never to be parted from thy side.
Guard me when the foe assails me;
Guide me when my feet shall fail me;
Bid me come to thee above,
With thy saints to sing thy love, forever and ever.
Amen.

# An Act of Faith

O my God, I firmly believe that thou art one God in three divine persons, Father, Son, and Holy Ghost; I believe that thy divine Son became man, and died for our sins, and that he will come to judge the living and the dead. I believe these and all the truths which the Holy Catholic Church teaches, because thou has revealed them, who can neither deceive nor be deceived.

# An Act of Hope

O my God, relying on thy almighty power and infinite mercy and promises, I hope to obtain pardon of my sins, the help of thy grace, and life everlasting, through the merits of Jesus Christ, my Lord and Redeemer.

# An Act of Charity

O my God, I love thee above all things, with my whole heart and soul, because thou art all-good and worthy of all love. I love my neighbor as myself for the love of thee. I forgive all who have injured me, and ask pardon of all whom I have injured.

# The Angelus

The angel of the Lord declared unto Mary.
   ℟. And she conceived by the Holy Ghost.
   Hail, Mary…
Behold the handmaid of the Lord.
   ℟. Be it done unto me according to thy word.
   Hail, Mary…
And the word was made flesh.
   ℟. And dwelt among us. Hail, Mary…
Pray for us, O holy Mother of God.
   ℟. That we be made worthy of the promises of Christ.

# *Hail, Holy Queen*
## (SALVE REGINA)

Hail, holy Queen, Mother of mercy, hail, our life, our sweetness and our hope. To thee do we cry, poor banished children of Eve: to thee do we send up our sighs, mourning and weeping in this vale of tears. Turn then, most gracious Advocate, thine eyes of mercy toward us, and after this our exile, show unto us the blessed fruit of thy womb, Jesus, O merciful, O loving, O sweet Virgin Mary! *Amen.*

# *Memorare*

Remember, O most gracious Virgin Mary, that never was it known that any one who fled to thy protection, implored thy help or sought thy intercession, was left unaided.

Inspired with this confidence, I fly unto thee, O Virgin of virgins my Mother; to thee do I come, before thee I stand, sinful and sorrowful; O Mother of the Word Incarnate, despise not my petitions, but in thy clemency hear and answer me. *Amen.*

# Make Me an Instrument
## of Your Peace
### (SAINT FRANCIS PRAYER)

Lord, make me an instrument of Your peace. Where there is hatred, let me sow love; where there is injury, pardon; where there is doubt, faith; where there is despair, hope; where there is darkness, light; where there is sadness, joy.

O, Divine Master, grant that I may not so much seek to be consoled as to console; to be understood as to understand; to be loved as to love; For it is in giving that we receive; it is in pardoning that we are pardoned; it is in dying that we are born again to eternal life.

# Prayer to My Guardian Angel

Angel of God, my guardian dear, to whom his love commits me here, ever this night be at my side, to light and guard, to rule and guide. *Amen.*

# Grace

**BEFORE:** Bless us, O Lord! and these thy gifts, which we are about to receive from thy bounty, through Christ our Lord. *Amen.*

**AFTER:** We give thee thanks for all thy benefits, O Almighty God, who livest and reignest world without end. Amen. May the souls of the faithful departed, through the mercy of God, rest in peace. *Amen.*